Northwest

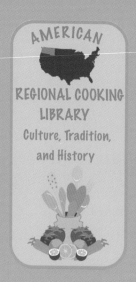

AMERICAN

REGIONAL COOKING
LIBRARY
Culture, Tradition,
and History

Northwest

Mason Crest Publishers

Philadelphia

Mason Crest Publishers Inc.
370 Reed Road
Broomall, Pennsylvania 19008
(866) MCP-BOOK (toll free)
www.masoncrest.com

First printing
1 2 3 4 5 6 7 8 9 1

Library of Congress Cataloging-in-Publication Data

Libal, Joyce.
  Northwest / [compiled by Joyce Libal ; recipes by Patricia Therrien ; recipes tested and prepared by Bonni Phelps].
     p. cm. — (American regional cooking library)
  Includes bibliographical references and index.
  ISBN 1-59084-619-2
 1. Cookery, American—Pacific Northwest style. I. Therrien, Patricia. II. Title. III. Series.
  TX715.2.P32.L53 2005
  641.59795—dc22
                              2004010522

Compiled by Joyce Libal
Recipes by Patricia Therrien
Recipes tested and prepared by Bonni Phelps
Produced by Harding House Publishing Services, Inc., Vestal, New York.
Interior design by Dianne Hodack.
Cover design by Michelle Bouch.
Printed and bound in the Hashemite Kingdom of Jordan.

Contents

Introduction
by the Culinary Institute of America

Cooking is a dynamic profession, one that presents some of the greatest challenges and offers some of the greatest rewards. Since 1946, the Culinary Institute of America has provided aspiring and seasoned food service professionals with the knowledge and skills needed to become leaders and innovators in this industry.

Here at the CIA, we teach our students the fundamental culinary techniques they need to build a sound foundation for their food service careers. There is always another level of perfection for them to achieve and another skill to master. Our rigorous curriculum provides them with a springboard to continued growth and success.

Food is far more than simply sustenance or the source of energy to fuel you and your family through life's daily regimen. It conjures memories throughout life, summoning up the smell, taste, and flavor of simpler times. Cooking is more than an art and a science; it provides family history. Food prepared with care epitomizes the love, devotion, and culinary delights that you offer to your friends and family.

A cuisine provides a way to express and establish customs—the way a food should taste and the flavors and aromas associated with that food. Cuisines are more than just a collection of ingredients, cooking utensils, and dishes from a geographic location; they are elements that are critical to establishing a culinary identity.

When you can accurately read a recipe, you can trace a variety of influences by observing which ingredients are selected and also by noting the technique that is used. If you research the historical origins of a recipe, you may find ingredients that traveled from East to West or from the New World to the Old. Traditional methods of cooking a dish may have changed with the times or to meet special challenges.

The history of cooking illustrates the significance of innovation and the trading or sharing of ingredients and tools between societies. Although the various cooking vessels over the years have changed, the basic cooking methods have remained the same. Through adaptation, a recipe created years ago in a remote corner of the world could today be recognized by many throughout the globe.

When observing the customs of different societies, it becomes apparent that food brings people together. It is the common thread that we share and that we value. Regardless of the occasion, food is present to celebrate and to comfort. Through food we can experience other cultures and lands, learning the significance of particular ingredients and cooking techniques.

As you begin your journey through the culinary arts, keep in mind the power that food and cuisine holds. When passed from generation to generation, family heritage and traditions remain strong. Become familiar with the dishes your family has enjoyed through the years and play a role in keeping them alive. Don't be afraid to embellish recipes along the way – creativity is what cooking is all about.

Northwest Culture, History, and Traditions

The first people arrived in the Northwestern states approximately 13,000 years ago, crossing from Siberia to Alaska by way of the Bering Strait. These first people of the country left an important record of their life and interaction with nature in the form of pictographs (simple drawings about daily life) on canyon walls. Some groups, such as the Puyallup and Chinook, lived on the western side of the Cascade Mountains where they were fishermen as well as hunters. Others, like the Nez Perce and Cayuse, lived on the plains and valleys to the east of the Cascades.

Many centuries passed before Spanish explorers discovered the northwest corner of North America in the sixteenth century and claimed the area for Spain. When George Vancouver began exploring the coast and Puget Sound in the late 1700s, he in turn claimed the area for England. The British arrived on a quest for "the great river of the west." The American Captain Robert Gray discovered the river near the end of the eighteenth century.

Thomas Jefferson was excited by the discovery of the Columbia River, and in 1804, decided to send explorers Meriwether Lewis and William Clark on a secret mission to explore the area. The trip had to be kept a secret because Lewis and Clark would be venturing into British territory. A Shoshone woman named Sacagawea and her French-Canadian husband, Toussaint Charbonneau, accompanied the exploration party as interpreters and guides. Lewis and Clark claimed the territory on behalf of the United States.

Fur trappers came to the Northwest in the early 1800s, but American settlers did not begin to arrive in great numbers until the 1840s. Some came by ship, but about a half million arrived by crossing over 2,000 miles of rugged terrain from Missouri to Oregon via the Oregon Trail, a journey that could take as long as six months. Some were attracted by fertile soil and favorable growing conditions while others were lured by the discovery of gold. This caused many tragic Indian battles, including wars with the Nez Perce, Modoc, and Paiutes. After years of valiantly fighting the American

army for their rights, American Indians were forced onto reservations, while 320 acres was offered for free to each male settler of European descent who wanted it.

Traveling the Oregon Trail was an extreme ordeal, and one out of ten who attempted it died along the way. While they traveled, pioneers ate foods such as bison steak and other game. Women cooked with wild onions, mushrooms, gooseberries, and other foods they found along the trail or provisions they brought with them in covered wagons. Even though nonwhite immigrants could not become citizens, and Chinese immigration was not legalized until 1868, many Chinese people began to immigrate to the Northwest because of hardships in their homeland. In fact, the first non-Indian fishermen in the Puget Sound area were Chinese. Initially lured there by gold strikes, they began to work as loggers, on railroad construction crews, in salmon canneries, and in the oyster industry. Unfortunately, in 1915, a law was passed that made it illegal for Asian people to engage in commercial fishing.

In the 1870s, railroads began to arrive in the Northwest, which brought many more settlers to the area. Washington's population grew from 1,000 in 1850 to 350,000 by 1890. After Hawaii became a state in 1898, many Japanese people who were working on sugar plantations there began to move to the Pacific Northwest. Others came directly from Japan.

Many Chinese and Japanese immigrants began to harvest fruit for a living. Filipinos also moved to the area and obtained jobs in fish canneries and agriculture. By World War II, Japanese immigrants and their descendants were growing almost 75 percent of the vegetables and most of the berries produced in Washington. Immigration continued into the twentieth and twenty-first centuries. In 1980, for example, two-thirds of the Asians in Washington State were born outside of the United States in countries such as Cambodia, Vietnam, and Laos. A census conducted in the 1990s showed that more than 50 percent of the people living in Seattle were born elsewhere.

Today, the Northwest is one of the most important agricultural areas in the United States. Washington produces more apples, pears, sweet cherries, red raspberries, dried peas, lentils, and spearmint than any other state in the Union. The Northwest is also a land of pioneers and immigrants who brought their histories and food preferences with them and then melded them with available resources. You'll sample a taste of the cuisine they developed when you use the recipes in this book.

Before you cook...

If you haven't done much cooking before, you may find recipe books a little confusing. Certain words and terms can seem unfamiliar. You may find the measurements difficult to understand. What appears to be an easy or familiar dish may contain ingredients you've never heard of before. You might not understand what utensil the recipe calls for you to use, or you might not be sure what the recipe is asking you to do.

Reading the pages in this section before you get started may help you understand the directions better so that your cooking goes more smoothly. You can also refer back to these pages whenever you run into questions.

Safety Tips

Cooking involves handling very hot and very sharp objects, so being careful is common sense. What's more, you want to be certain that anything you plan on putting in your mouth is safe to eat. If you follow these easy tips, you should find that cooking can be both fun and safe.

Before you cook...

- Always wash your hands before and after handling food. This is particularly important after you handle raw meats, poultry, and eggs, as bacteria called salmonella can live on these uncooked foods. You can't see or smell salmonella, but these germs can make you or anyone who swallows them very sick.
- Make a habit of using potholders or oven mitts whenever you handle pots and pans from the oven or microwave.
- Always set pots, pans, and knives with their handles away from counter edges. This way you won't risk catching your sleeves on them—and any younger children in the house won't be in danger of grabbing something hot or sharp.
- Don't leave perishable food sitting out of the refrigerator for more than an hour or two.
- Wash all raw fruits and vegetables to remove dirt and chemicals.
- Use a cutting board when chopping vegetables or fruit, and always cut away from yourself.
- Don't overheat grease or oil—but if grease or oil does catch fire, don't try to extinguish the flames with water. Instead, throw baking soda or salt on the fire to put it out. Turn all stove burners off.
- If you burn yourself, immediately put the burn under cold water, as this will prevent the burn from becoming more painful.
- Never put metal dishes or utensils in the microwave. Use only microwave-proof dishes.
- Wash cutting boards and knives thoroughly after cutting meat, fish or poultry — especially when raw and before using the same tools to prepare other foods such as vegetables and cheese. This will prevent the spread of bacteria such as salmonella.
- Keep your hands away from any moving parts of appliances, such as mixers.
- Unplug any appliance, such as a mixer, blender, or food processor before assembling for use or disassembling after use.

Metric Conversion Table

Most cooks in the United States use measuring containers based on an eight-ounce cup, a teaspoon, and a tablespoon. Meanwhile, cooks in Canada and Europe are more apt to use metric measurements. The recipes in this book use cups, teaspoons, and tablespoons—but you can convert these measurements to metric by using the table below.

Temperature
To convert Fahrenheit degrees to Celsius, subtract 32 and multiply by .56.

212°F = 100°C
(this is the boiling point of water)
250°F = 110°C
275°F = 135°C
300°F = 150°C
325°F = 160°C
350°F = 180°C
375°F = 190°C
400°F = 200°C

Liquid Measurements
1 teaspoon = 5 milliliters
1 tablespoon = 15 milliliters
1 fluid ounce = 30 milliliters
1 cup = 240 milliliters
1 pint = 480 milliliters
1 quart = 0.95 liters
1 gallon = 3.8 liters

Measurements of Mass or Weight
1 ounce = 28 grams
8 ounces = 227 grams
1 pound (16 ounces) = 0.45 kilograms
2.2 pounds = 1 kilogram

Measurements of Length
¼ inch = 0.6 centimeters
½ inch = 1.25 centimeters
1 inch = 2.5 centimeters

Pan Sizes

Baking pans are usually made in standard sizes. The pans used in the United States are roughly equivalent to the following metric pans:

9-inch cake pan = 23-centimeter pan
11x7-inch baking pan = 28x18-centimeter baking pan
13x9-inch baking pan = 32.5x23-centimeter baking pan
9x5-inch loaf pan = 23x13-centimeter loaf pan
2-quart casserole = 2-liter casserole

Useful Tools, Utensils, Dishes

basting brush

blender

flour sifter

meat thermometer

muffin pan

nut chopper

omelet pan

pastry cutter   pie plate   pizza pan   ring mold

rolling pin   vegetable grater   vegetable strainer   wire whisk

Cooking Glossary

cream A term used to describe mixing sugar with butter or shortening until they are light and well blended.

cut Mix solid shortening or butter into flour, usually by using a pastry blender or two knives and making short, chopping strokes until the mixture looks like small pellets.

dash A very small amount, just a couple of drops or shakes.

dollop A small mound, about 1 or 2 tablespoons.

fillets Thin strips of boneless fish or meat.

knead To work dough with the hands, lifting the far edge, placing it upon the rest, and pushing with the heal of the hands.

mince Cut into very small pieces.

sauté Fry in a skillet over high heat while stirring.

set When a food preparation has completed the thickening process and can be sliced.

shucked Seafood (such as oysters, clams, or mussels) with the shell removed.

simmer Gently boiling, so that the surface of the liquid just ripples gently.

whisk Stir briskly with a wire whisk.

zest A piece of the peel of lemon, lime, or orange that has been grated.

Special Northwest Flavors

apples

cherries

cinnamon

cranberries

hazelnuts

maple syrup

pears

nutmeg

mint

salmon

Northwest Recipes

Apple-Yogurt Muffins

Preheat oven to 350° Fahrenheit.

Ingredients:

1 cup grated apple
3 cups flour
1¼ cups sugar
3½ teaspoons baking powder
½ teaspoon salt
¼ teaspoon nutmeg
½ teaspoon orange zest
2 eggs
one 8-ounce container vanilla yogurt
1 cup butter or margarine
1 teaspoon cinnamon

Cooking utensils you'll need:
measuring cups
measuring spoons
vegetable grater
2 mixing bowls
wire whisk
1 or 2 muffin pans (depending on how large you make the muffins)
paper cupcake liners
small saucepan
small, shallow bowl
basting brush

Directions:

Place paper liners in the muffin cups. Wash and grate unpeeled apple(s) to measure 1 cup, and set it aside. Put the flour and 1 cup of the sugar in a mixing bowl. Stir in the baking powder, salt, nutmeg, and orange zest. **Cut** in ¾ cup butter, and set it aside. Whisk eggs in the second mixing bowl. Stir in the yogurt and grated apple. Pour the apple mixture into the flour mixture, and stir just enough to combine. Divide the batter evenly among muffin cups, and bake for 20 to 25 minutes (until muffins are completely done). When cool enough to handle, remove muffins from pan. Meanwhile, mix the remaining sugar with cinnamon in the shallow bowl. Melt remaining butter in the small saucepan. Working with one muffin at a time, brush the top with melted butter, and then dip the top in the sugar mixture.

Tips:

Unless instructed to do otherwise in a recipe, always use large eggs for baking.

To reduce fat in recipes calling for yogurt, always use low-fat or no-fat varieties.

Add ½ cup chopped nuts to these muffins, if desired.

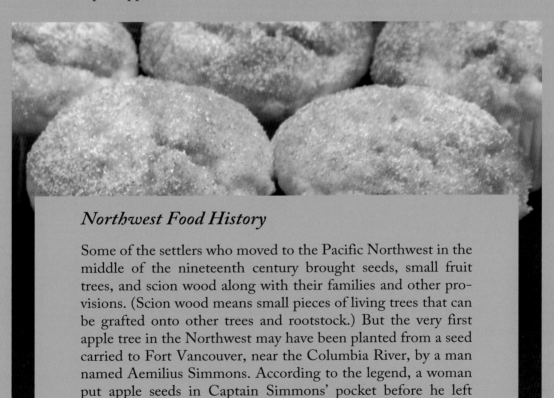

Northwest Food History

Some of the settlers who moved to the Pacific Northwest in the middle of the nineteenth century brought seeds, small fruit trees, and scion wood along with their families and other provisions. (Scion wood means small pieces of living trees that can be grafted onto other trees and rootstock.) But the very first apple tree in the Northwest may have been planted from a seed carried to Fort Vancouver, near the Columbia River, by a man named Aemilius Simmons. According to the legend, a woman put apple seeds in Captain Simmons' pocket before he left London in the early 1820s. After reaching Fort Vancouver, he gave the seeds to a man named John McLoughlin. He in turn gave the seeds to his gardener, who planted them.

Microwave Applesauce

Now you can make delicious homemade applesauce in record time.

Ingredients:

8 apples
⅓ cup water
¼ cup sugar
1 teaspoons lemon zest
1 teaspoon vanilla
¼ teaspoon cinnamon
¼ teaspoon nutmeg

Cooking utensils you'll need:
measuring cups
2-quart microwave-safe dish
lid for the dish (or plastic wrap)

Directions:

Peel and core the apples, cut them into small chunks, and place them in the microwave-save dish. Add the water, and cover with the lid or plastic wrap. Using the high setting on the microwave, microwave for about 12 to 15 minutes. Check to see if the apples have become tender. If not, microwave for a couple more minutes. When the apples are tender, mix in the sugar, zest, vanilla, and spices. Microwave for 2 or 3 more minutes (until the sugar dissolves). Mash or puree the applesauce, as desired, and serve either warm or cold.

Northwest Food History

The first commercial apple crop in the Pacific Northwest was grown by Henderson Lewelling and his partner William Meek—and believe it or not, people say those apples sold for as much as $5 each! Here's how it happened: When Mr. Lewelling moved his family to the territory by way of the Oregon Trail in 1847, one of the covered wagons he brought with him was filled with hundreds of small fruit trees, including cherries, pears, and other fruits as well as apples. According to the story, the wagon was so heavy it required several pairs of oxen to pull it. William Meek, who later married Mr. Lewelling's daughter, came to the Northwest carrying apple seeds. The men formed a partnership, and their first apple crop matured during the California gold rush. The men took the apples to these miners, who were so excited to have the opportunity to eat fresh fruit that they were willing to pay a fortune for each apple.

Northwest Food History

Josiah Red Wolf was a member of the Nez Perce tribe, a group of American Indians who lived in the Northwest and fought the United States Army for many years. Like the other Native American people in the area, they lost their battle to maintain their territory. Josiah Red Wolf is said to have been the last survivor of his people's war. He planted apple trees near the Snake River—leaving behind a sweet legacy as a reminder of bitter loss.

Baked Maple-Pecan Apples

Pecans add crunch and maple syrup adds delicate sweetness to these baked apples.

Preheat oven to 350° Fahrenheit.

Ingredients:

2 apples
2 tablespoons chopped pecans
2 tablespoons raisins
¼ teaspoon cinnamon
2 tablespoons water
4 teaspoons maple syrup
2 tablespoons butter

Cooking utensils you'll need:
apple corer
measuring cup
measuring spoons
small baking dish
nut chopper (optional)
small mixing bowl
aluminum foil

Directions:

Beginning at the stem end of the apples, remove most of the core, but do not remove the bottom of the core at the blossom end. Leaving this part intact will prevent the ingredients placed in the core cavity from leaking out of the bottom of the apple. Peel just the top stem end of each apple (about ⅓ of the way down the apple), and place them in the baking dish. Place the chopped nuts in the small bowl, and stir in raisins and ⅛ teaspoon cinnamon. Place the mixture in the apple core cavities. Push 1 tablespoon of butter into each apple cavity. Put the water into the baking dish. Drizzle 2 teaspoons maple syrup into each apple cavity and over the unpeeled portion of the apples. Bake for 30 minutes (until apples are tender), sprinkle with the additional cinnamon, and serve warm.

Tip:

Add a small scoop of vanilla ice cream to each apple, if desired.

Berry Cherry Smoothie

Make a delicious fruit smoothie for breakfast or any time of the day

Ingredients:

1½ cups cran-cherry juice
1½ cups fresh or frozen whole strawberries
1½ cups fresh or frozen pitted dark sweet cherries

Cooking utensils you'll need:
measuring cup
blender

Directions:

Pour the juice into the blender container, add the cherries and berries, and puree. This is enough for 2 servings.

Tips:

Add crushed ice or ice cubes to the container before pureeing, if desired.

Add yogurt for extra protein, if desired.

You can substitute canned pitted sweet cherries for the fresh or frozen ones. Drain before using, and add several ice cubes.

Northwest History

Chinese immigration to the Pacific Northwest decreased with the passage of the Chinese Exclusion Act in 1882. Among other things, this law banned Chinese women from immigration. By 1890, there were forty Chinese men in the United States to each Chinese woman. In 1907 and 1908, the United States refused to allow Japanese men to immigrate, but did allow women, relatives, and children of those already living here to do so. The 1924 National Origins Act restricted Asian immigration for four decades. In some areas of the Northwest, Asians were prevented from owning or even renting land. European settlers were even known to expel Chinese, Japanese, and Filipino people from some areas. In 1942, during World War II, Congress passed a law ordering all Japanese people removed from coastal areas, with the exception of Hawaii. Most of these people were American citizens, yet they were deprived of their constitutional rights. Concentration camps were established in Idaho, California, and five other states to intern Japanese citizens. Yet, many Japanese-Americans volunteered for military service, and their units were among the most decorated in military history. It was not until 1966 that some of the anti-alien land laws were repealed, and in 1988, the United States Congress apologized for the internment.

Crab Omelet

Ingredients:

4 eggs
1 tablespoon olive oil
1 small onion, **minced**
1 cup Dungeness crabmeat
1 tablespoon grated Parmesan cheese
1 tablespoon minced parsley.

Cooking utensils you'll need:
measuring cup
measuring spoon
mixing bowl
wire whisk
skillet, non-stick pan, or omelet pan
spatula

Directions:

Put the oil in the skillet, add the onion, place over medium heat, and cook until the onion is tender. *Whisk* the eggs in the mixing bowl. Stir in crabmeat, and parsley. Pour the mixture over the onions, and reduce heat. Cook the egg mixture without stirring. As the outside edges of the omelet begin to solidify, lift the edges gently to let the uncooked portion run beneath the omelet. When the center of the omelet has *set*, slide the omelet onto a serving plate, gently lift one side, fold the omelet in half, garnish with parsley, and serve.

Tip:

Sauté sliced green onion, small pieces of red or green pepper, *minced* broccoli, or other vegetables that you enjoy, and place them on the omelet before folding it in half. If you cannot locate Dungeness crabmeat, substitute another variety.

Northwest Food Facts

Dungeness crab is named for Dungeness, Washington, which is where this particular variety was first harvested. Dungeness crab was the first shellfish to be commercially harvested on the North Pacific Coast, and it remains the only crab that has commercial importance in Washington State. Human beings aren't the only ones who love to eat this crustacean; it is also a preferred food of octopus.

Oregon is home to the largest cheese factory in the world.

Oregon was the first state to ban nonreturnable bottles and cans, having passed a law against them in 1971.

Cranberry Mousse Salad

Cranberries are one of North America's three commercially grown native fruits. (The other two are blueberries and concord grapes.) This long-lasting berry is rich in vitamin C and was an important part of the diet for some American Indians.

Ingredients:

One 20-ounce can crushed pineapple
1 cup water
One 6-ounce package strawberry or raspberry
   JELL-O®
One 16-ounce can whole-berry cranberry sauce
3 tablespoons lemon juice
1 teaspoon nutmeg
2 cups low-fat sour cream
½ cup chopped pecans

Cooking utensils you'll need:
measuring cups
measuring spoons
nut chopper (optional)
vegetable strainer
mixing bowl
saucepan
ring mold
serving plate that is larger than the ring mold

Directions:

Place the strainer over the bowl, and drain the pineapple. Pour the juice into the saucepan (reserving the crushed pineapple). Add the water to the pineapple juice, place over medium heat, and bring to a boil. Immediately stir in the JELL-O®, and remove from heat. Stir in the cranberry sauce, lemon juice, and nutmeg. Place the mixture in the refrigerator, and allow it to chill until partially thickened. Stir in the sour cream, pecans, and pineapple. Pour the mixture into the ring mold, and refrigerate until *set*.

Tip:

To unmold the salad, dip the mold into hot water for just a moment, wiggle the mold gently to loosen the gelled salad, place the serving plate upside-down on top of the ring mold, invert the plate and ring mold, set the plate down, and gently lift the ring mold.

Northwest Food History

Cranberries were an important food for the Queet and Quinault Indians who lived near the Columbia River. Indians used the fruit when making pemmican, a pounded blend of meat, fat, and berries. This nutritious food was dried in the sun and carried on long voyages. When Lewis and Clark wintered over in the area, they purchased cranberries from the Indians. The first commercial cranberry bog was established in 1885, and it is still yielding an annual crop. In Coos County, Oregon, where this bog is located, growing cranberries is sometimes referred to as "mining for red gold."

Charles McFarlin, the man who started this first bog did not just use cranberries that were already growing in the area. Instead, he brought plants with him from Cape Cod, Massachusetts. He used them to develop a new berry (called the McFarlin) that is still being grown by many commercial growers today.

Chinese immigrants built the first commercial bogs in Oregon, and Queet and Quinault Indians harvested the crops. In 1946, Ocean Spray established a facility at Bandon, Oregon. Today, a half dozen companies process cranberries in the area.

Cranberries grown in the Northwest are particularly dark in color due to the long growing season. Because of this desirable feature, they are mixed with those grown in other parts of the country in order to enhance the color of the finished product.

Walla Walla Pizza

This pizza is named for sweet Walla Walla onions that take their name from the Walla Walla Valley in Washington where they are grown.

Preheat oven to 425° Fahrenheit.

Ingredients:

One 12-inch pre-baked pizza shell (see "Tip")
2½ tablespoons olive oil
1 pound sliced sweet onions (Walla Walla variety if available)
¼ cup chopped and drained sun-dried tomatoes (variety that is packed in oil)
½ teaspoon oregano
½ teaspoon thyme
½ teaspoon basil
salt and pepper to taste

Cooking utensils you'll need:
measuring cup
measuring spoons
cookie sheet

Directions:

Put the pizza shell on the cookie sheet. Arrange the onions on the pizza shell, and drizzle olive oil over them. Add the sun-dried tomatoes, and sprinkle herbs across the top. Add a couple shakes of salt and pepper, and bake for 10 minutes (until onions are tender and beginning to turn golden brown).

Tip:

If you would like to make your own pizza shell, here's an easy recipe: Put 1½ cups of very warm water in a large mixing bowl, and sprinkle one package of active dry yeast over it. Stir to dissolve the yeast, and then stir in 1 of cup flour and ½ teaspoon salt. Stir in 2½ additional cups flour. Now use your hands to knead the dough adding up to ½ cup of additional flour, as necessary. (Be careful to not add too much flour as it can make the pizza dough stiff and dry.) Rub a little olive oil around in the bowl, place the pizza dough in the bowl, swirl it around to cover the bottom with oil, and then turn it upside down so that the oiled surface is on top. Cover the bowl with a clean towel, and set it somewhere warm for about an hour. Then oil the cookie sheet or a pizza pan, use your hand to punch the dough down, and spread it in the pan. Bake the pizza for 10 or 15 minutes at 450° Fahrenheit, and then proceed with the recipe above. To make your pizza shell even more nutritious, substitute 1 cup of whole wheat flour for 1 cup of the white flour.

Salmon Barbecue

Wild salmon from the Pacific Northwest contains important omega-3 fatty acids and is one of the most nutritious foods you can eat.

Ingredients:

2 large onions, sliced
1 large salmon fillet
butter
salt and pepper
brown sugar

Cooking utensils you'll need:
aluminum foil

Directions:

Wash the salmon, and pat it dry with paper towels. Make a double layer of aluminum foil on your countertop, being certain that it is longer than the salmon fillet. Spread half of the onion slices along the length of the aluminum foil. Place the salmon on the onion slices. Use your hands to rub a small amount of butter on the salmon. Add a *dash* of salt and pepper. Sprinkle lightly with brown sugar, and place the remaining onions on top. Put a double layer of aluminum foil on top of the salmon, and seal well by crimping the edges of the top and bottom foil pieces together. Place the salmon package over hot coals, cook for 10 minutes, and check to see if the fish flakes easily. If not, reseal the package and continue cooking. You may want to flip the package over to better cook the second side.

Tip:

For a flavor alternative, add a couple shakes of teriyaki sauce and thinly sliced lemons to the fish before adding the final layer of onions.

Northwest Food Facts

Once in its lifetime, each salmon leaves the ocean and makes an incredible journey in order to mate and lay eggs in the same freshwater stream in which it was born. Some swim for nearly a thousand miles upriver and leap over rocks and small waterfalls to elevations of over 6,000 feet (1,828.8 meters) above sea level to reach their goal. This dramatic annual migration of salmon marked the changing seasons for many American Indians living in what is now Idaho, Oregon, and Washington State. This enduring symbol of the Pacific Northwest was extremely important to several tribal cultures. Today, the number of salmon is in decline. Overharvesting, the building of dams that interfere with migration, excessive demand on limited water resources, and destruction of habitat all play a role in this problem.

Gingered Salmon

Along with high-quality protein and omega-3 fatty acids, salmon offers vitamins A, B, and D, as well as calcium, iron, magnesium, zinc, phosphorus and potassium. Health professionals suggest eating fish twice a week.

Ingredients:

3 tablespoons soy sauce
1 teaspoon sesame oil
2 teaspoons honey
1 tablespoon dry cooking sherry
1 cup chicken broth
2 teaspoons minced ginger
1 garlic clove
4 salmon fillets (approximately 4 ounces each)

Cooking utensils you'll need:
measuring cup
measuring spoons
garlic press
mixing bowl
plastic wrap
broiler-safe pan

Directions:

Wash the fillets, and pat them dry with paper towels. Put the soy sauce in the mixing bowl. Stir in the sesame oil, honey, sherry, chicken broth, and ginger. Use the garlic press to press the garlic over the mixture. (If you don't have a garlic press, mince the garlic.) Place the fillets in the mixture, cover with plastic wrap, and refrigerate for 2 hours. Then broil the fillets for 8 minutes (or until the fish flakes easily). The rack should be approximately 6 inches from the heat source.

Tips:

To reduce the amount of fat and salt in this meal, use lite soy sauce and fat-free reduced-sodium chicken broth.

This dish can also be cooked on an outdoor grill.

Northwest Food History

Salmon was an extremely important food source for many of the Indians living in the Northwest. Believing the first salmon that they caught each season was very special, they reserved it for a ceremony. During the ceremony, the head of the fish was placed upstream so future salmon would understand which way to travel. Many Indians believed this was necessary to assure the return of the salmon. While men speared the fish, women were in charge of cleaning and drying it. To extract oil from the salmon (which was used for both cooking and medicine) a canoe was partially buried in sand and then half filled with dead fish and water. Hot rocks were placed in the water to make it boil. As fish oil rose to the surface, women skimmed it off.

Oyster Stew

The Pacific Northwest has only one native oyster. Olympia oysters are small but meaty and mild yet flavorful.

Preheat oven to 350° Fahrenheit.

Ingredients:

½ cup milk
½ cup light cream (half and half)
2 cups **shucked** oysters
½ teaspoon paprika
2 tablespoons butter
1 cup heavy cream (whipping cream)
salt and pepper to taste
¼ cup **minced** parsley

Cooking utensils you'll need:
measuring cups
measuring spoons
vegetable strainer
saucepan
skillet

Directions:

Place the strainer over the saucepan, and drain the shucked oysters. Set the oysters aside. Add the milk, light cream, and paprika to the oyster liquid, place over medium heat, and bring to a **simmer**, stirring constantly. Meanwhile, put the butter in the skillet, place it over medium heat, add the oysters, and heat until the oysters are hot. Transfer the oysters and butter to the saucepan, stir in the heavy cream, and continue heating and stirring until the stew begins to simmer. Stir in the minced parsley, and add salt and pepper to taste. Garnish with parsley sprigs, if desired.

Tips:

If you would like to reduce the fat in creamed soups and chowders, such as this oyster stew, substitute non-fat milk for some of the light and heavy cream.

This recipe calls for oysters that have already been shucked. If you decide to shuck fresh oysters, wash them first. Then put a heavy glove on the hand you'll use to hold the oyster. Use an oyster knife, screwdriver, or can opener in the other hand to open the oyster. Remove each oyster from its shell.

Northwest Food Facts

Three introduced oyster varieties are now being raised in the Pacific Northwest along with Olympia. Originally from Japan, the Kumamoto is sweet and juicy. Interestingly, this oyster is now extinct in its homeland. The Pacific oyster, another introduced species from Japan, has been raised in Washington since the beginning of the twentieth century. The remaining variety is called the European flat. Oysters are often sold using the name of the place where they were raised, such as Pearl Bays, Westcott Bay, Snow Creek, and so on. The coastal waters of the Pacific Northwest are extremely well suited to oyster raising and produce "bivalves" of exceptional taste and texture.

Halibut & Shrimp Bake

During the nineteenth century, fishing for halibut was a dangerous activity. This bottom-dwelling fish was in deep water that was sometimes very rough. Luckily, all it takes is a quick trip to the grocery store for you to net all of the ingredients to make this uncomplicated dish.

Preheat oven to 350° Fahrenheit.

Ingredients:

3 cups water
dash salt and pepper
2 cups fresh corn (see "Tip")
2 pieces of halibut (each about 1¼ pounds)
1½ cups shrimp
2 tablespoons butter

Cooking utensils you'll need:
measuring cups
measuring spoon
saucepan
baking pan

Directions:

Wash the halibut, and pat it dry with paper towels. Wash the shrimp, and remove the shells and black "vein." Pour the water into the saucepan, and add a dash of salt and pepper. Bring the water to a boil over high heat, and add the corn. Bring it to a boil again, reduce heat, and *simmer* for 10 minutes. Use a little of the butter to grease the bottom of the baking pan. Layer the halibut and shrimp in the pan. Pour the corn and water mixture on top, and place the remaining butter in the pan. Bake for 30 minutes (until halibut flakes easily).

Tip:

To cut corn off the cob, hold it upright and steady with the stem side down. With a sharp knife in your other hand, slice downward, cutting off a few rows of corn kernels. Then go back and gently scrape that area of the cob to get more of the corn juice. Some people like to place the cob in the center tube of an angel-food cake pan so the cut kernels fall into the pan. You still need to hold the cob steady as you cut when using this method. If fresh corn is not available, use frozen corn.

Northwest Food History

Early American Indian fishermen were sometimes concerned about the types of mysterious creatures that might live under the sea. Halibut themselves are rather mysterious looking since both of their eyes are on the right side of their body. Ranging in size from ten to five hundred pounds, these wide flat fish can live up to fifty-five years and grow up to eight feet long (2.4 meters). Meat from another interesting looking creature, the octopus, was the preferred bait for catching halibut. Specialized fishing hooks were often decorated with elaborate carvings of shaman, fish, or birds, both to attract the halibut and for protection against the unknown.

Northwest Food History

The specialized hooks used by Indians who fished in Northwest coastal waters helped provide much needed food for Indian families while also working to preserve the abundant halibut supply. Indians made the hooks large enough so that small halibut could not swallow them. It was also undesirable to catch a fish that would be too large to place in the dugout canoes that were used for fishing. Therefore, a fishing hook's barb was made so that it could not pierce a fish that was too large. In this way, a good number of fish were always unharmed, preserving a healthy breeding stock.

Halibut Crunch

French-fried onions add nice textural contrast to the soft baked halibut in this dish.

Ingredients:

butter
3 tablespoons cooking oil
1½ teaspoons lemon juice
¼ teaspoon garlic salt
⅛ teaspoon pepper
¼ teaspoon marjoram
⅛ teaspoon dry mustard
4 halibut fillets
⅔ cup canned French-fried onions
3 tablespoons grated Parmesan cheese

Cooking utensils you'll need:
measuring cup
measuring spoons
mixing bowl
plastic wrap
baking pan

Directions:

Wash the fish, pat it dry with paper towels, and set it aside. Put the cooking oil and lemon juice in the mixing bowl, and stir in the garlic salt, pepper, marjoram, and dry mustard. Place the filllets in the mixture, turn them over to be certain all sides are coated, cover the bowl with plastic wrap, and refrigerate for 20 minutes.

Preheat oven to 450° Fahrenheit. Butter the baking pan, and place drained fish in it. Crumble the French-fried onions on the fish, and top with Parmesan cheese. Bake for 20 minutes (until fish flakes easily).

Pork Loin with Hazelnut Stuffing

Preheat oven to 450° Fahrenheit.

Ingredients:

1 to 1½ pounds boneless pork loin (about 3 inches thick)
1½ cups dried bread crumbs
¾ cup chopped hazelnuts
¾ cup grated Parmesan cheese
3 tablespoons butter, softened
1½ tablespoon mustard
3 garlic cloves
3 teaspoons fresh chopped rosemary
1½ teaspoons sage
½ teaspoon salt
⅛ teaspoon pepper

Cooking utensils you'll need:
measuring cups
measuring spoons
mixing bowl
garlic press
shallow baking pan
meat thermometer

Directions:

Mix bread crumbs, nuts, and cheese in the mixing bowl. Stir in the softened butter and mustard. Use the garlic press to squeeze the garlic over the mixture. (If you don't have a garlic press, *mince* the garlic.) Stir in the rosemary, sage, salt, and pepper, and set the stuffing aside. Wash the pork, pat it dry with paper towels, and trim off any excess fat. Lay the pork flat, and slice (between 2 and 2½ inches deep) down the entire length of the meat. Then make a horizontal slice from the cut you already made to within ½ inch of the edge of the roast. Repeat on the other side of the first cut, and open up the roast. Spread half of the stuffing on the bottom (mid section) of the opened roast.

Fold the top of the roast back over the stuffing, and carefully place the roast in the baking pan. Use your hands to pat the remaining stuffing over all exposed areas of the roast, insert the meat thermometer near the center of the roast, and bake for 20 minutes. Then reduce heat to 350º Fahrenheit, and continue baking for another 20 minutes (or until the meat thermometer reaches 160º Fahrenheit). Remove the roast from the oven, and allow it to rest for 10 minutes before slicing.

Tip:

If necessary, substitute 1 teaspoon crumbled dried rosemary for the fresh rosemary.

Northwest Food History

Also called filberts, hazelnuts belong to the birch family. Although the hazelnut tree normally grows into a ten- to fifteen-foot shrub, hazelnuts are pruned to one stem and look like trees in the Pacific Northwest. A man named Felix Gillet brought hazelnuts from Europe to California in the 1870s. Nursery stock from Mr. Gillet's orchard was used to establish the nuts in Oregon.

Years ago, people thought hazelnuts had mystical powers. Some people buried them because they thought that would increase their power of clairvoyance. Other people used the wood for divining rods to search for valuable minerals in the soil.

Northwestern–Style Pear Pie

Ingredients:

For the crust:
1 cup flour
½ teaspoon salt
¼ cup chopped walnuts or pecans
⅓ cup shortening
2 tablespoons very cold water

For the filling:
2 pounds fresh pears
2 tablespoons flour
2 tablespoons butter
½ cup dark corn syrup
¼ cup brown sugar, packed
1 tablespoon lemon juice
7 walnuts or pecans

For the topping:
½ cup brown sugar, packed
⅓ cup flour
½ teaspoon cinnamon
¼ cup butter
¼ cup chopped walnuts or pecans

Cooking utensils you'll need:
measuring cups
measuring spoons
flour sifter
nut chopper (optional)
mixing bowl
pastry blender or 2 butter knives
rolling pin
wooden cutting board or other flat surface
saucepan
9-inch pie plate

Directions:

Step 1: Sift 1 cup flour and the salt into the mixing bowl, and stir in ¼ cup chopped nuts. *Cut* in shortening until the mixture looks like coarse meal. Cut in the water until well mixed. If necessary, add up to 1 additional tablespoon of water. Use your hands to form the dough into a ball, sprinkle some flour on the wooden cutting board or another flat surface, place the dough upon it, and flatten it a little with your hand. Rub some flour onto the rolling pin, and roll the dough from the center toward the outside edges, working your way around the circle. Add more flour to the rolling pin, and lift the edge of the dough and place more flour under it, as necessary. When the circle of dough is large enough for the pie plate, fold it in half, set the pie plate next to the dough, place the dough in the pie plate, and open the dough. Pat the dough gently into the plate, cut off any large areas of dough that are hanging off the edges so there is about the same amount all around the pie, and crimp the edges, folding any remaining excess dough down and against the inside edge of the pie plate.

Step 2: Preheat oven to 400° Fahrenheit. Wash, peel, core, and slice the pears. Set 6 slices aside for the top of the pie, and place the remaining pears in the mixing bowl. Sprinkle with 2 tablespoons of flour, mix well, and pour pears into the pie shell. Melt 2 tablespoons butter in the saucepan, stir in corn syrup, ¼ cup brown sugar, and lemon juice. Continue cooking until warmed through, and pour the mixture over the pears. Place the reserved pears and 7 nuts on top of the pie, arranging the pears in a circle with nuts between them. Place the remaining nut in the center.

Step 3: Mix together ½ cup brown sugar, ⅓ cup flour, and the cinnamon. Cut in ¼ cup butter until well combined. Stir in ¼ cup chopped nuts, sprinkle the mixture on pie, and bake for 55-60 minutes.

Tip:

To save a little time, you can use a prepared piecrust. Sprinkle ¼ cup chopped nuts on the bottom of the pie shell, and pat them a little with your hand before making the pear filling.

Northwest Food History

Pears, one of the world's oldest cultivated fruits, are the number-one tree fruit crop grown in Oregon and the number-two tree fruit crop in Washington State. These two states combined produce more than 650,771 tons of pears annually.

    Pears first arrived on the eastern shores of North America with early colonists and were brought to the Pacific Northwest in the 1800s. The varieties grown in Oregon and Washington today are the same as the early varieties grown in Belgium and France.

Cherry Upside–Down Cake

Preheat oven to 375° Fahrenheit.

Ingredients:

7 tablespoons butter
1 cup brown sugar, packed
2 eggs
1 cup white sugar
½ cup milk
1 cup flour
¼ teaspoon salt
1 teaspoon baking powder
2 cups pitted sweet cherries

Cooking utensils you'll need:
cookie sheet
oven-proof skillet or
9-inch square baking pan
saucepan
measuring cups
measuring spoons
electric mixer
2 mixing bowls
serving plate or platter
(larger than the skillet or baking pan)

Directions:

Place the cherries in a single layer on the cookie sheet, and place in freezer until ready to use. (Having the cherries slightly frozen helps to prevent them from rising up into the cake as it bakes, but do not let the cherries freeze solid.) Place 5 tablespoons of the butter in the skillet (or another pan), and place over low heat until butter is melted. Stir in brown sugar, continue cooking until sugar is dissolved, set the skillet aside. Melt the remaining butter in the saucepan, stir in the milk, and set it aside. Put the eggs into one of the mixing bowls, add the sugar, and beat 4 minutes. Gradually mix milk mixture into the egg mixture, and set it aside. Put the flour into the remaining mixing bowl, and stir in salt and baking powder. Pour the flour mixture into the egg mixture. Beat just until well combined. Place cherries on top of the brown sugar layer in the skillet or baking pan. Pour cake batter over the cherries, and bake for 40 minutes (or until done). Immediately place a serving plate or platter upside down on top of the cake pan. Invert the plate and pan so that the plate is right side up with the cake pan on top of it, and remove the cake pan. Serve the cake warm or cold, and add a scoop of ice cream, if desired.

Tips:

To see if a cake is done, insert a toothpick in the center of the cake. If there are no crumbs on the toothpick when you remove it, the cake is done.

To make a pink cake, substitute ½ cup cherry juice for the ½ cup milk.

Northwest Food History

Cherries were one of many fruits that came to North America with early settlers. In the 1600s, cherry pits were already being planted in the eastern part of the country. Henderson Lewelling, the same man who is credited with the arrival of apples and pears in the Pacific Northwest, brought cherries across the Oregon Trail in 1847. Lewelling Farms' first commercial sweet cherry crops began ripening several years later. Today Oregon and Washington produce approximately sixty percent of the nation's sweet cherry crop. Ninety-five percent of the sweet cherries grown in the Pacific Northwest are Bing, Lambert, and Rainier varieties. Bing cherries, the most famous of the sweet varieties, was named after a Chinese immigrant who worked at Lewelling Farms. This famous orchard is also credited with developing the Lambert cherry. Rainier also originated in the Northwest, having been developed at the Washington State University Research Station.

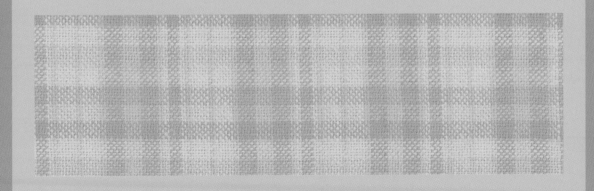

Chocolate–Hazelnut Sweet Pizza

Ninety-nine percent of the hazelnuts produced in the United States come from Oregon's Willamette Valley.

Ingredients:

one 6-ounce jar maraschino cherries
1 pound white almond bark (or white chocolate chips)
one 12-ounce package semi-sweet chocolate chips
2 cups miniature marshmallows
1 cup hazelnuts
1 cup Rice Krispies®
3 tablespoons quartered green cherries
½ cup coconut
1 teaspoon cooking oil

Cooking utensils you'll need:
measuring cups
measuring spoons
2 saucepans
12-inch pizza pan (or other pan)

Directions:

Butter the pizza pan, and set it aside. Drain the maraschino cherries, cut each one in half, and set them aside. Set about 2 ounces of almond bark aside, and place the remaining amount in the saucepan. Add the chocolate chips, and place over low heat. Cook until melted, stirring constantly, then remove from heat. Stir in marshmallows, hazelnuts, and Rice Krispies®. Spread the mixture on the pizza pan, arrange the cherries on the chocolate mixture, and sprinkle coconut over the top. Put the oil in the second saucepan with the remaining almond bark. Melt over low heat, stirring constantly, and drizzle over the pizza. Chill in the refrigerator until the chocolate is firm, but then store the pizza at room temperature.

Northwest Food History

Maraschino and green cherries are purchased in jars, but they begin their life as regular sweet cherries. After being pitted, they are placed in sweet, flavored syrups. Maraschino cherries were first made in Italy and Yugoslavia. In the 1890s, they were exported to North America, where they were served in fancy restaurants. By 1896, American cherry producers were trying to make their own version of these cherries. The first maraschino cherries were placed in liqueur, but American producers gradually decreased the amount of liqueur used until none was present at all. Instead, they used almond flavoring. Green cherries are made with mint flavoring. Color is also added to these cherries.

Northwest Food Facts

Fiber-filled hazelnuts contain lots of essential nutrients, including vitamin E, phosphorous, iron, protein, and folate. According to health research, hazelnuts may help reduce your risk for cardiovascular disease. Like other nuts, hazelnuts are high in monounsaturated fat, which can help reduce LDL (the "bad" cholesterol) and total blood cholesterol levels when eaten as part of a diet low in saturated fat. Be careful of how many nuts you eat, however. Because they are so small and taste so good, it's easy to eat a lot of calories really fast. One and a half ounces per day are all you need to reap the positive benefits.

Frosted Hazelnuts

Preheat oven to 275° Fahrenheit.

Ingredients:

2 eggs
2 tablespoons water
1 cup sugar
½ teaspoon cinnamon
½ teaspoon cloves
½ teaspoon allspice
4 cups hazelnuts

Cooking utensils you'll need:
measuring cup
measuring spoon
mixing bowl
wire whisk
2 cookie sheets or jelly roll pans
waxed paper

Directions:

Grease the cookie sheets and set them aside. Separate the egg whites from the yolks, placing the whites in the mixing bowl. Use the yolks for another purpose. *Whisk* the egg whites and water, add the sugar, cinnamon, cloves, and allspice, and whisk again. Let the mixture stand for 5 minutes, then whisk again, and stir in the nuts. Spread the nuts on the prepared pans, and bake for 50 to 60 minutes (until the nuts are crispy). Pour the nuts onto waxed paper, and allow them to cool. Store unused nuts in containers with tight-fitting lids.

Frozen Mint Cups

Ingredients:

1 small box vanilla wafers
2 squares unsweetened chocolate
1 cup butter
2 cups plus 1 tablespoon confectioners' sugar
  (powdered sugar)
2 teaspoons vanilla
4 eggs
¾ teaspoon peppermint flavoring
whipping cream

Cooking utensil you'll need:
18 paper cupcake liners
cookie sheet
heavy-duty plastic bag
rolling pin
measuring cup
measuring spoon
saucepan
mixing bowl

Directions:

Place the cupcake holders on the cookie sheet, and set them aside. Put the vanilla wafers into the plastic bag, and use the rolling pin to crush them. Place 1 tablespoon of the crumbs into each cupcake holder. Put the chocolate in the saucepan, place it over low heat, and cook until melted. Cream butter and 2 cups confectioners' sugar in the mixing bowl. Stir in melted chocolate and vanilla, and beat well. Add the eggs one at a time, beating well after each addition. Stir in the peppermint flavoring, and divide the mixture evenly into the cupcake holders. Divide the remaining wafer crumbs evenly among the cupcake holders, and place them in the freezer until ready to serve. Whip cream with the remaining 1 tablespoon confectioners' sugar to soft peaks. (Be careful not to over beat, or you may end up with buttermilk with little chunks of butter floating in it.) Top each mint cup with a dollop of whipped cream just before serving.

Northwest Food History

Mint was brought to North America by early Massachusetts colonists who used it to flavor bad tasting medicines. Over the years, mint, like America's settlers, began to move west. Today Oregon, Washington, and Idaho grow much of North America's mint supply.

Ninety percent of mint oil produced in the United States is used for chewing gum, toothpaste, and sweet items such as candies. Leaves are used for tea and other drinks as well as for garnishes. Mint also has nonfood uses such as for insect repellents and aroma therapy, as well as for chewing tobacco and compost.

Minted Citrus Cooler

Begin to make this fruity beverage eight hours before you'd like to serve it.

Ingredients:

2 cups unsweetened pink grapefruit juice
1 cup sweetened orange juice
⅓ cup sugar
1 cup loosely packed fresh mint leaves
1 cup lemon-flavored sparkling water, chilled
additional mint sprigs for garnish (optional)

Cooking utensils you'll need:
measuring cups
mixing bowl
plastic wrap
small wire-mesh strainer
pitcher

Directions:

Stir grapefruit juice, orange juice, sugar, and mint leaves together in the bowl. Cover with plastic wrap, and place in the refrigerator for 8 hours. Place the strainer on top of the pitcher, strain the juice mixture as you pour it into the pitcher, and discard the mint. Stir the sparkling water into the juice just before serving. Garnish each glass with a mint sprig.

Northwest Food Fact

Starbucks—the largest coffee chain in the world—started in Seattle.

Further Reading

Atkinson, Greg. *The Northwest Essentials Cookbook: Cooking With the Ingredients That Define a Regional Cuisine*. Seattle, Wash.: Sasquatch Books, 1999.

Desmond Stang, Kathleen. *Northwest Berry Cookbook: Finding, Growing, and Cooking with Berries Year-Round*. Seattle, Wash.: Sasquatch Books, 1998.

Gunderson, Mary. *The Food Journal of Lewis & Clark: Recipes for an Expedition*. Yankton, South Dakota: History Cooks, 2003.

Kafka, Barbara, Sharon Kramis, and Schuyler Ingle. *Northwest Bounty: The Extraordinary Foods and Wonderful Cooking of the Pacific Northwest*. Seattle, Wash.: Sasquatch Books, 1999.

Kelly, Denis. *Pacific Grilling: Recipes for the Fire from Baja to the Pacific Northwest*. Seattle, Wash.: Sasquatch, 2003.

Preus, Mary. *The Northwest Herb Lover's Handbook: A Guide to Growing Herbs for Cooking, Crafts, and Home Remedies*. Seattle, Wash.: Sasquatch Books, 2003.

Schreiber, Cory. Wildwood: *Cooking from the Source in the Pacific Northwest*. Berkeley, Calif.: Ten Speed Press, 2000.

Williams, Jacqueline B. *The Way We Ate: Pacific Northwest Cooking, 1843–1900*. Pullman, Wash.: Washington State University Press, 1996.

For More Information

Idaho History
www2.state.id.us/gov/fyi/history/index.htm

Idaho Timeline
www.idahohistory.net/dateline.html

Kitchen Safety
www.premiersystems.com/recipes/kitchen-safety/cooking-safety.html

Lewis and Clark
www.pbs.org/lewisandclark/

Oregon History
www.ohs.org/education/oregonhistory/index.cfm

State Agricultural Profiles
www.agclassroom.org

State History
www.theus50.com

Washington State History
www.historylink.org

Publisher's note:
The Web sites listed on this page were active at the time of publication. The publisher is not responsible for Web sites that have changed their addresses or discontinued operation since the date of publication. The publisher will review and update the Web sites upon each reprint.

Index

Author:

In addition to writing, Joyce Libal has worked as an editor for a half dozen magazines, including a brief stint as recipe editor at *Vegetarian Gourmet*. Most of her experience as a cook, however, has been gained as the mother of three children and occasional surrogate mother to several children from different countries and cultures. She is an avid gardener and especially enjoys cooking with fresh herbs and vegetables and with the abundant fresh fruit that her husband grows in the family orchard.

Recipe Tester / Food Preparer:

Bonni Phelps owns How Sweet It Is Café in Vestal, New York. Her love of cooking and feeding large crowds comes from her grandmothers on both sides whom also took great pleasure in large family gatherings.

Consultant:

The Culinary Institute of America is considered the world's premier culinary college. It is a private, not-for-profit learning institution, dedicated to providing the world's best culinary education. Its campuses in New York and California provide learning environments that focus on excellence, leadership, professionalism, ethics, and respect for diversity. The institute embodies a passion for food with first-class cooking expertise.

Recipe Contributor:

Patricia Therrien has worked for several years with Harding House Publishing Service as a researcher and recipe consultant—but she has been experimenting with food and recipes for the past thirty years. Her expertise has enriched the lives of friends and family. Patty lives in western New York State with her family and numerous animals, including several horses, cats, and dogs.

Picture Credits